Teardrops from Rose Petals

by Rose Hometchko

DORRANCE
PUBLISHING CO
EST. 1920
PITTSBURGH, PENNSYLVANIA 15238

Dorrance Publishing Co
585 Alpha Drive
Suite 103
Pittsburgh, PA 15238
Visit our website at *www.dorrancebookstore.com*

ISBN: 978-1-6386-7019-3
eISBN: 978-1-6386-7968-4

Dedication to my daughter, Rose Hometchko

Happy Birthday, Rose

3/26/71 — 6/17/09

Memorial to Scooter

You saw what others could not see
With avian telepathy.
My color draining out to
An alabaster sculpted sight.
A battery without a spark
A tire with a pinhole mark.
As the tomb replaced the bed
You breathed your soul into my head.

For her parrot, who passed

Thank You, Scooter

3/15/07

Thank you for everything.
Thank you for my high-density glossy life
Radiant like solar rays.
Days pass.
Thank you for each car ride caper,
Adventures in secret hiding places.
Dry rubber kisses, and nibbles and itches.
You even licked tears from my wet eyelashes
when tragedy rained.
Thank you for your quiet content,
Peace to be, Simply, with me.
And your exit, a silent retreat,
Your last comfort, my subtle heartbeat
Thank you for keeping me somewhat earth-bound.
When it is you who should be flighted.

Scooter

I wonder sometimes if I let those beautiful wings glide
Would I lose my friend?
Thank you for all sensual things,
delicate like your downy fluff,
a weightless puff of snowflake white,
Or vibrant like your rosy cheeks,
A rainbow trail to your tail,
A cropped, ragged, rugged vein.
And where have you found your liberation?
Do I spy the skies for ghosts who fly?
Do I search the earth for a surreal perch?
As in life, you are in death,
On me, in me, eternally.
Your Grand finale, a pilgrimage,
The end, beginning. Thank you for being part of me.

Feathers

Fluff, a powder puff white and airy
Sent as if from a fairy pool
Spiny veins from wings
Strong yet fragile things
I leave them both upon the floor
Swirling underfoot I can't ignore

Eulogy for Gram, My Rock

5/18/06

The coffee mug and candlewick
Displayed their heat
In curly-cues
Of sooty hues.
Untimely news:
A ring in monotone.
Remote voice in same sad drone
To italicize what I knew
I felt
I dreamt
I prayed.

Quiet Death closed her eyes,
(A kiss to bestow her demise)
And let her blindly to arise
And follow,
Flying fearless,
Fleeing frivolous bonds
Body-bound.
From here to there,
Without a sound,
Sleeping Beauty soars.

Tangled in a knotted head,
Like so much yarn.
Un-crocheted until this day,
her introduction to Sir Necros
his universal invitation,
froze Madam Chaos in her steps.

I proudly hold your best creation,
In fertile weeping willow hues,
Close to my own head—ironic!
Obsessive mental clarity
And antiseptic worldly views.
In its perfect regularity,
My security in variegated wool strands,
Lives the comfort of your dexterous hands.

My guardian, angelicin your simple grace,
I still have your visage.
I study your face
In my humblest moments.
Thanks to You
I have all the strength I need.
You gave that to me.
But more than that,
You Gave me You
unconditionally

Yoga

Is the search for the *unique* part of you
a passion
a puzzle
a secret
a romance
Inside you
It keeps you awake late at night,
It makes you a STAR,
It's something you couldn't live without,
How did you live before?
(with one eye open?)
A love
INFINITE
distant and strong
-greater than any I person could bear-
of all things
with all you have to give

The Teacher

I-Rose

I am middle C
the home, the point of reference.

I am the conduit
passing knowledge on to others
who do not know.

Initially I tried exploring
aggressively pursuing new worlds and
each time I hovered over the abyss
almost falling.

I tried absorbing
passively tasting the fruits of other's labor
watching and waiting
lulled into senselessness.

Now I am perfectly suited
to quickly watch and learn then act,
learn more than act
living and showing and telling
those who may someday
explore
or learn
or teach.

Rose was a teacher, lab tech, and yoga and meditation teacher.

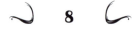

Besides teaching yoga and meditation, Rose also worked as a teacher and lab technician at Luzerne Community College. Just thought you might get to know Rose as a person.

1977-78

Miss McCarthy, my 2nd-grade teacher, met with Mom about skipping grade 3. I was transferred from grade 3 to grade 4. She told my mom I handed in all my workbooks completed by October. It was an incredible experience since Western culture pairs age with responsibility and opportunity. So my teaching career started out in limbo. I realize I had to bide my time until I could teach professionally.

Just being was not an option, I had to move to doing. The only real job I had was to go to school to learn and observe teachers. I enjoyed that part. The difficulty, which made much of my childhood a serious endeavor, was to be the best at whatever I do so my efforts led to a tumultuous onward and upward adventure.

Fall

School has begun.

The slightest sway in the atmosphere, from nonchalant
summer to pre-hibernative autumn. We can feel the
shift, from body to head, from motion to sombre
stillness, from thermal glare into dim.
I snap to attention as the chalk hits my hand, new
asphyxiation games, high on dust and permanent
marker stench.

They look *at* me, *to* me, *for* me as pillar, as mountain, as
treasure chest opened, spewing answers and answering
prayers. I know so little of all there is! But a galaxy
more than they do! Still, the facade draws them near,
and peaked ears turn for their destiny, written in
formulas, numbers and Greek symbols scattered on hard
black-backed slate stage.

The details, in stale pages, made palatable by droll
bookworm sages, makes heads even larger than egos
would fill. And so, in the seats, like calves suckling
teats, they (kink in the knowledge that flows from my
tongue, from my head, from my heart).

I hope at the end of the day, of the book, they have felt
our time was worth every demand—and the wealth in
their heads a fortuitous brand.

Besides her journals when she was 8 years old until the 2000s, then the last
years were on her computer.

Sunset

2/8/08

Through skeletal trees
I saw the red
It swelled and glowed
And warmed the sky.

Sun, thespian
Cannot slip down
Like drops of blood
From open wounds.

It flashes bright
Nightfall
Without a stage

An eye to seek
Applause in stares

Breathing sighs
Its smooth descent
O'Hara-esque
Named the same

Reveals a train
Of orange gold
Fading to blue-black
Like coal

Sequined with studs
And shiny shapes
The evening makes
A curtain call.

To Mom

6/9/03

Good people have a hard time accepting things from others. You are a perfect example. You have a difficult time with compliments, with gifts, with touching. You want to "do it yourself." So that you don't have to bother anyone. This is a noble attitude, but eventually, all your work takes its toll on your body and mind, so that a crisis knocks you out.

More

8/18/03

There is nothing more
Just yourself

If you can't find it in you
To take charge
Take care of you
Then reality is beyond your comprehension.

.

Change

6/15/03

It is in change that I excel, I adapt.
My deformity or gift—my superpower is my overgrown brain.
I transform, I change, I die with stagnation,
Work and rest in cycles forever.
My perfection, is not laser focus
But in making myself fit anywhere.
By adapting I make imperfect things perfect for me. I am my own
creator of quality—I set the rules and standards.
In accepting flaws we see where the best qualities start.

Challenge

6/09/03

It seems like our world is falling apart—wars, unemployment, layoffs, terrorism—and on a smaller scale—companies downsizing, reduced healthcare, a sudden rise in divorces and separations among people we know saddled with lots of bills. Your own personal issues such as your life's goals and career need close attention. Even the weather can break us if we are already feeling in dire straits.

It is times like this that we try to get more involved so we understand what is happening to us. Our minds and bodies can only handle so much stress before it begins to break down. Before that happens we need to shelter ourselves to find out what we don't need, what we want, and what is garbage. We need to do spring cleaning in our head in order to make room for ME. It's not selfish to do things for yourself as long as you take care of the rest of the bits and pieces that make up your life. You need to balance yourself before you can juggle your life.

Sometimes you find it difficult to pull yourself away from what you love, but it is necessary to test yourself. Eventually you will come back. It is like muscles—work and rest for the rest of your life. Although it may not be easy, but neither is the alternative which is losing strength every day until you die. You know how your life differs from others so you decide on a path and work toward it—that makes you focused and stable. Occasionally you need to take a break from your routine to appreciate the stable path you have chosen. You take your body and mind out of the comfort zone and then bring it back.

16

Yoga Lesson

I seek my body's advice in fuzzy times

I read my hair today—
If parted on the left I guess it's Rose with pretty bows
And flower shows and painted toes.

I read my hips today—
They stretched on the left again
It's Rose with to & fro of vivid prose as breathing flows.

I read my heart today—
It opened in the center so I guess some parts do not close.
My heart is open to
Ideas, critiques, compliments.

Power of Ten

2003

America stands out from all other countries in many ways, but strangely enough, in the way we count our stubborn nature won't allow us to follow a completely natural system of measurement—the Metric System. This universal group of units—liter, meters, grams and other equally foreign terms—is simply a conglomeration of tens.

Sometime ago, some very bright person looked as far as his or her fingertips for a standard way to measure things. The previous method of measuring had been dependent on the relative size of a King's body. The foot, for instance, was really the length of a foot! What happened when that monarch left the throne? New foot, new size. And imagine if the society became a matriarchy??It certainly would make the thumb on the deli scale look like a needle in a haystack, when considering how merchants had to change their concept of size. So someone picked and object and made it THE LENGTH UNIT. End of story. When we count metric we count in tens hundreds, thousands (decameter = 10 meters kilometer = 10 meters). The organization and simplicity of ten is beautiful.

Happy Mother's Day

May 2003

The essential notion for everyone to understand is that mothers try to do the best that they can with what they have. When I think of how you nurtured me, sacrificing selflessly, enduring unpleasant experiences, I cannot give enough thanks for a perfectly healthy beginning. From the stories of the dreaded "liver for dinner," Lamaze classes, nutritious meals with abundant vitamins and protein to the superlative efforts to address my medical needs, I am truly grateful for your good work and hope to represent the health, wellness, and strength you strove for in me. With deepest sincerity I give you the **biggest thank-you**.

Cycles

We love cycles. From bicycles to spinning rides at an amusement park, we like to see a beginning and an end. When we start, nourish and complete a task, this is true contentment and pride. The feeling is like making bread from scratch—from the sifting of the flour to the heavenly bites of the tasty loaf. This is goodness in action. Yoga class is like baking. We start with our breath, manipulate it, then let go— a cycle.

Why Do We Cry?

To release
To celebrate the end of a mission
To punctuate the end of a growth cycle
Our degree of emotion at the time reflects an attachment to that
which we release.
Our type of emotion reflects what growth is next for the outpouring in
question

LIFE—you give you take
ART—you think, you make
LOVE—you remember, you fake, in your heart a little earthquake
RUMORS—you hear, you ignore
QUESTIONS—you volley, you store
ADVICE—you dodge, you deplore; always seeking a little more
CRYING—you empty, you release
LAUGHING—you smile, you deceive
THINKING —you enlighten, you receive
LIES AND TRUTH—a seamless wave

Scars

5/9/05

Some are big
Some are small
Some don't even hurt at all
Skin is poked, pierced, scratched, stretched, bitten, broken
Bruise and burn—bleed and weep
Pain prevents a peaceful sleep

3/19/09

Celebrate the joy of life against the background of death
Rose passed away 6/17/09

Breath

Each puff will ward off death
At the ending

Tricycle

Big third wheel
Guiding little two

A perfect trio
Like "I love you"

Women Raising Themselves

Inspiration

I decided to analyze my female role models with the goal of understanding myself and my influences, my habits and interests. In doing so I realized that most of these women were without children or past the years during which they actively had to raise them. In essence, these women were only responsible for their own growth and self-expression which comes with self-knowledge. They could offer me more than I think they could imagine. I was the eager receptive student. I thank them for their unique way for being there to shape me into who I am today.

Beauty

Beauty as defined by a wise old man.

An old man to his wife:
"Oh my God! Hold me back—a redhead."

To his wife:
"You're beautiful."

Wife's response:
"Thank you."

Single Red Rose

I cradle you to my nose
And move you to a lying pose
Next to me.

Your petals open wide with ease
Like a dancer's legs performing tease

Your bud is coiled and pristine
Surrounded in red velveteen
A rose unfolding.

The fragrance, subtle and profound,
Arouses her without a sound
Smell fantastic

Unscreened

Everyone needs a constant
Either mind, body or spirit.
I've tried focusing on them all.
The most important to me is a stable mind.

Less Is More

Ageless   Boundless
Unless   Nameless
You Stress   Faceless
Priceless   With Useless
Timeless   Impedes Progress

Age 8

11/17/08

Aren't we all?
Yes, a costumed child
In a world warped until
Suddenly tall
With gray in the hair and wrinkles in the stare.
Time won't stall
But we play like kids
Games a parent forbids.

How Did I Know

At the age of eight I was fully developed (for United States culture, that is). I had to reach the level of maturity of my mom so that we could do things together. This is not to say that my mom is the intellectual equivalent of an eight-year-old. Rather, I chose to spurt as fast as humanly possible, for me eight years out of the womb.

Can you imagine the burden of being an adult child? Doogie Howser had an outlet for his energies in med school, whereas I, being in nature a teacher, had no one to teach. Well, not really. Having skipped second grade, I used to make workbooks for my friends in third and fourth grade; this was quite remarkable in its expedience. (This was confirmed by my teacher

Cervical Cancer

2009

The entrance to infinity lies in the cervix.
A room with no view
A seductive vestibule
A strange alternative
Vacant and roomy
Not blushed and flushed
With blood-colored decor.
A nest in unrest, infertile at best
A pit with a bite
A wound but not wounded, rather wound around you.

Star Child

Precious child, what a joy.
Raised on Spock,
Enterprising more or less.
"Watch!" "Look" "Listen"
My first words and favorite still.

Did That Hurt?

Pain is an illusion
Pleasure is a delusion—
A metronome keeps the pace
Which we name life.
The space between LIFE
Is one or the other.
At the edge it divides
The divine from the mortal
The alive from the corpses. I can smile and
Silently shake my head "NO"

Infinity

Me
You, too
Club taboo.
Kabuki
Fire
You inspire
To the pyre
However spooky.
We create
Open the gates
Locksmith
With a new key.
It's not a place
It's a journey to take.
I'm the whisper you strain to hear
I'm the shudder you strain to fear.
I'm the echo you cannot find.
It's not a sound
It's the call to awake!

Cheater

Rose & Me
2003

I think I was pretending I didn't see your lies
My love for you hid the truth I didn't want to see.
I gave you years you spent in a day.
I brought you the sun which you bent the rays
No gesture of love was good enough for you
You had to reap more than you sowed.
I was left in a field of weeds
A victim of my selfless deeds.

Inside

3/7/03

What do you give birth to every day?
A pregnant pause before a revelation?
A swollen hand from repetitive toil
A tender foot which pedals on terra firma?

How do you take care of your child?
Do you wash in purest water?
Do you feed from nature's pantry?
Do you wrap in secure cloth

How do you nurture your proudest gift?
Do you wear it like a badge?
Do you tinker and toy with it? Do you give it time to grow?

I must be quite verbose
When I could have asked,
"What makes you alive?"

Summer of '89

What do you do when words don't get through to the people you love
And who loves you.
Are you always trying to restrain your crying
Are you ashamed on yourself relying
While walking on Lehigh Street thinking through, "with a little
help from my friends."

You were told as a child to be good for goodness' sake
For goodness is the path to heaven
But did they ever tell you to suffer—it's not pleasant.
And the "practice what you preach" rule is still in effect.

Yet to live is to suffer in a hell called earth
Merely to live it is to have eternal life.

Fall '89

There is a time late at night when things change.
It is a change from dark to light
A sudden transition.
My smile evens, my eyebrows elevate,
My teeth hug each other
As a new thought appears, I guess I am just sentimental
And it is wise to rise above.
They are thoughts of a secure past and unrequited LOVE.

But why does he escape when I come near?

The robins flee when I offer them bread.
I cannot touch their feathers of brown
What reason do they have to stop their song?

The answer, it seems, is quite clear.
Since they have seen man's destruction
The trust once possessed has disappeared.

Loneliness

Why is the world afraid of a dreamer?
Ideas never thought of hurt the mortal pride.

Alone but Not Lonely

Perhaps I am selfish, I want the best for me
I never meant to hurt anyone.
I was born alone: I grew up alone.
My peers were few, adults my entertainment.

There is a time late at night when things change.
It is a change from dark to light—
A sudden transition at that.
My smile evens, my eyebrows elevate,
My teeth hug each other
As the thoughts appear.
I guess I am just sentimental
And it is wise to rise above.
They are thoughts of a secure past of unrequited love

Twenty Years Old

5/11/91

A score is what I am,
But it feels like dog years to me.
Responsibility—that's an ugly word
Especially when I want to be
Unbothered by daily life—
I want to be free.
If I had a magic lamp
I have one fantasy:
To live in truth and wisdom and love
Devoid of travesty.
After twenty years I am finally cheerful
But the eyes of my family are wet and tearful.

1981 Christmas - Present First Diary
Beginning of Rose's Long-term Journal Writing

January 1, 1981

We are going to have company tonight. My friend Marian might come over also. I hope I can go outside; I want to bury my catfish. Their names are Heckle and Jeckle.

January 3, 1981

Today I went to Barbison School of Modeling. We did informal modeling and talked after we did our nails in the P.M. session. Mommy and I put on the 7 basic beauty tips.

January 20, 1981

Today Laura and I went to Drama class. We go every Tuesday. After Drama we went to Silver Queen to eat. We played the jukebox. I played 3 songs and Laura played 5.

January 22, 1981

Today Mommy and I went to the Holiday Inn, where we will be modeling. After that we went to the Arena for a buffet. The salad bar was about 8 feet long.

January 25,1981

Today I was in the fashion show and I found a dollar bill at the door. It started late because the girl screwed up the names.

January 29,1981

Today Mommy and I went to Kung Fu classes in Wilkes-Barre. We finished the Tiger Form. All together there are 10 steps and I know them all.

Hot Potato

When I have time to be alone
To decide, to direct, I suffer.
I cause my own suffering.
Events spiral down in a whirlpool of misery
An unredeemable time in us

It's like a game of hot potato.
I don't want the suffering,
I don't want to hold the hot potato anymore.
I need to pass it on.
We all have the duty to hold it or pass it on.

One Step at a Time

Have you ever been disappointed
That the result of your efforts went awry,
Like the cheesecake you made is perfect—
Except for the big hole down the center.
Now needs to be covered
By a decorative Hershey Kiss.

Especially disheartening are the efforts
We put into people
Who let us down.
Ah! There's the key—expectation;
The source of great sorrow.
Step back from ourselves—
Our egos for a moment
And think about the last person
Who didn't fulfill a need.
???????

Real

8/8/03

I am real inside and out
I like real things
Things I can touch, things that grow.
I like real food, not processed
That provides me with my fuel.
Me and life
Raw, simple, ever present.

Purity

9/7/03

There is nothing so beautiful as the first snowfall.
White unblemished snow
And pure crystalized water.
Add the word natural and you have a marketing success.
So it is only natural that we look for purity in people.
Children are thought to be
Natural, untainted, pure, fresh and new.
Throughout life events and issues mark our purity
Our bodies are visible histories
Exhibiting our stresses, thoughts and
Intangible webs of ideas
Stuck to us with little hope of disentangling.
Yoga can help us regain our essence, our purity into the simplest part
of ourselves.
In a focused, relaxed state
We move with the ease of a child,
Casting away years of debris and contamination
Until breath and body flow as one
As we did when we made our debut on earth.

Now That I Have Your Attention

3/15/07

Lessons from the ether,
neither good or bad.
My teacher with a starry slate
illuminates me.
Showing what is in disguise
the jigsaw of infinity
piece by piece.

Truck Stop

8/29/07

She noticed the fake green leather seats
And sat in the booth—
Her favorite color—green.
She needed privacy, as much as could be had
In a truck stop.
She hoped to hear conversations—
Woes and laughs and histories
That would spark her imagination
Sleepless nights
At the truck stop
Templates she could idiom.
She did this frequently
When she could not sleep
In lieu of sleep with drowsy eyes,
pen falling out of her hand
like a drunk falling upstairs.
Sometimes a jackpot!
Other times dismal chatter
In colloquial clichés.
Today!
A new voice.

Male & Female

1/2 &½

Balance
Yin & Yang
Black & White
Life & Death
Blending of extremes regimes

YESTERDAY was not so long ago, at least in my memory. In fact, there are moments where time has not moved and I can easily recreate and capture past events as though they were in real time. As long as I have these precious memories you are just as alive as I recall each period of your life; these thoughts are what support me and carry me through each day. My yesterdays are forever etched in my heart and keep me strong. I can always review your photos on the computer or the albums. Of course, your Saki has been here since 2009. He is alive and well but I know you'd be disappointed since I spoil him. You loved your special parrots so I keep you in mind when I am with him. He does remember your commands so he has some structure.

TODAY and every day is just another time I go through the yesterdays and find delight in thoughts and memories that slip quietly into my into my heart and sustain me for another day. So many places and people generate times that I keep close to my heart. I know you would have used the social media like Facebook, and I am thankful to have so many of your friends participate in messaging me as well as post on your site: "In Loving Memory of Rose Hometchko." Some of them I do consider **OUR** friends.

TOMORROW, the future, I cannot anticipate. I loved you yesterday as my baby girl, as my daughter, my best friend and companion in our many adventures. Those memories will not end or diminish. You always will be a part of me. I know you and Gram will be waiting for me.

Preface
MJ Rose

Death is nothing at all. It does not count. I have only slipped away into the next room. Nothing has happened. Everything remains exactly as it was. I am I, and you are you, and the old life that we lived so fondly together is untouched, unchanged. Whatever we were to each other, that we are still. Call me by the old familiar name. Speak of me in the easy way which you always used. Put no difference into your tone. Wear no forced air of solemnity or sorrow. Laugh as we always laughed at the little jokes that we enjoyed together. Play, smile, think of me, pray for me. Let my name be ever the household word that it always was. Let it be spoken without an effort, without the ghost of a shadow upon it. Life means all that it ever meant. It is the same as it ever was. There is absolute and unbroken continuity. What is this death but a negligible accident? Why should I be out of mind because I am out of sight? I am but waiting for you, for an interval, somewhere very near, just 'round the corner. All is well.

From M J Rose (pen name)
Henry Scott Holland

Happy Birthday
Rosemary Hometchko

3/26/1971 - 6/17/2009

∞

I can never feel alone or separated
from you, especially on your
birthday. The private moments are
the times I am reminded we are
never apart because your spirit will
live deep within my heart. Saki
remembers most of the lessons
you taught him. He is now a part
of both of us. He is a connection
of the tender care of your love for
birds. My yesterdays make my
tomorrows easier since your spirit
lives deep within me. My life is more
purposeful and rich in so many ways
because of you. You taught me so
much about the world that I didn't
even think to explore and we did it
together. Some people think I am
wrong to call your name and speak as
though are present, but why because
you are not visible should I dismiss
the existence of the time you shared
with me here while you were visible.
Families are forever and will remain
together through eternity. Gram, You
and Me will be together once again.

This will be the eighth year I have
continued to celebrate your birthday,
but this year I found a student you
tutored and he will be honored to
share memories of you over dinner.
I really appreciate and cherish
people who keep thoughts of you
alive in their memories. Since he is
great with plants both a tea rose and
bamboo will be among the plants
in his front window. He thought
so highly of you, your patience in
teaching, your soft- spoken tone,
and your knowledge of the math he
was having some difficulty with. I
am grateful you left me with many
memories and people who are willing
to share time and emails with me.
Your true friends have become a part
of me too. Even though people don't
always last, their memories do.
Forever, Rose's Mom

One March 26 the highlight of my life came
A baby girl, **ROSE** was her name.
We would celebrate our birthdays- Rose and Kay
How could that happiness just slip away
For 38 years these celebrations would last
How quickly time has passed.

Shared events with my pride and joy I find
Are deeply embedded in my mind
Your hugs and kisses are deeply missed,
You'll find them on my wish list.
I treasure all your growing years
The memories bring happiness as well as tears.

As you grew I learned so much from you
I am still finding more of how much you knew.
You were involved in so much through life
(dance, drama, modeling, music, teaching
self-defense, yoga, meditation, and more)
Even when life presented you with times of strife.

You were my encourager and source of delight
You are the last memory I have at night.
"Hi, Mom, how are you!" A hug, laugh, smile
For any of these I'd run mile after mile.
Especially around these special days
I bear the loss of your warm, thoughtful ways.

My grief will turn to joy when we reunite
As I pass through the tunnel of light.
Meet me there with Gram that day
Three strong women-Gram, Rose and Kay.

Forever Rose's Mom

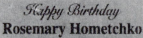

Happy Birthday
Rosemary Hometchko

2009 - 2019
A Decade
3,657 Days Passed

∞

The years, the days we could have
should have spent together
I cannot even imagine although
sometimes I try. At first I spent
the days of the recent past
and the times we had together.
Then I watched you deal with cancer,
so strong and brave on the outside
when I know you were distraught
inside yet not showing or
allowing others to see your pain
both physically and emotionally.
So strong just like Gram.

Never a day goes by when I
have reminders of you --
sometimes as a baby, other times
as a little girl. So many photos
are away to reconnect with your
high school and college days.
And of course your adult years --
You showed me many new ways
of doing things. I not only loved
by admired you. Someday three
strong women Gram, Rose
and Kay will be together again.

Forever Rose's Mom

Rose Hometchko

When you became an adult, our roles began to change. You were now not only my daughter but my go-to girl. I thought of you both as a companion and friend as well as my daughter. You were always on call for installing my ink for printers, setting my cordless phone for use, fine-tuning my computer as well as adjusting my VCR. You were so good at the mechanics what for me was New Age. Now I am easily lost.

Each day I have many **_REWINDS_**. I see a place, a photo or meet someone and my mind immediately recalls countless times we spent together. Your school and a couple college friends help ignite some of these memories. I treasure these wonderful people like you did at school. I wonder about your yogis at Danko's to whom you were so devoted.

Then I **_PAUSE_**. I reminiscence about the details of these shared events. They flood my thoughts. I take the opportunity to meditate and bring us back to happier periods of time. You are deep within my heart so I am never alone; you are a part of me. Love endures forever.

Then I **_FAST FORWARD_**. You would be so amazed and an expert at smartphones and especially Facebook. So many opportunities missed. So much you, we would enjoy and you would be proficient at doing. I miss you for so many reasons.

Love as Always, Rose's Mom
Happy Birthday, 2016

You might see a small reddish
(like your hair) cat following you
from the Rainbow Bridge. His
name is Sunshine. One day I came
home from clearing up your house.
I pulled the car on our driveway
and opened the door to the kitchen.
I notice him following me when I
got into the kitchen he laid down
on the floor and ALL the cats came
to greet him and it was like he
belonged here. I called him Sunshine
since I think he came in to comfort
me. I never saw him at your house
or here at my house but I felt a
close bond and a daily ritual
with you and me and Sunshine.
He helped me go through
the lonely times…Recently
he just passed away with
cancer. Look for him and take
care of him until I get there
with you.

Love Always, Forever
Rose's Mom

Happy Birthday, Rose

3/26/71 - 6/17/09

Each day brings me closer to you and Gram.

Wish there were some visiting privileges over the years. But find my own space and time to recall all the happy moments I spent with you. There seems to be more and more time to recall past adventures. When this happens I may be alone but not lonely. The memories are so clear like I am seeing videotape. This brings me a measure of happiness. The memories just come and may be times you were a baby, but as you grew there are also special times that I clearly recall from your school years to college and finally at your job at LCCC.

You might see a small reddish (like your hair) cat following you from the Rainbow Bridge. His name is Sunshine. One day I came home from clearing up your house. I pulled the car on our driveway and opened the door to the kitchen. I noticed him following me when I got into the kitchen, he laid down on the floor and ALL the cats came to greet him and it was like he belonged here. I called him Sunshine since I think he came in to comfort me. I never saw him at your house or here at my house but I felt a close bond and a daily ritual with you and me and Sunshine. He helped me go through the lonely times. Recently he just passed away with cancer. Look for him and take care of him until I get there with you.

Love Always, Forever Rose's Mom

Happy Birthday, Rose Hometchko

Years have passed, six to be exact
Since we celebrated our birthdays together
Another birthday I will celebrate
Knowing you will be with me in spirit.
You always were and will be are there with me.

I hear your voice in the distance
But I mourn for your touch, sight & sound
So the emptiness and loneliness remain.
Yet our spirits are forever entwined.

So much I continually learned from you
You taught me what a mother should be.
You made my days special and complete.
I treasure all the years of memories

As you grew you were my companion,
Encourager, and source of delight.
The one who knew me and cheered me on,
Your arms comforted me in sad moments.

Shared events with **my pride and joy**
Are deeply embedded in my mind.
Your hugs and kisses are deeply missed,
Especially around these special days.

"Hi, Mom! How are you?" A smile, a laugh,
A hug, a kiss and all our shared experiences
Are events that bonded us forever.
My grief will be joy when we reunite.

So much more is in my heart
Locked away, never to part
When my time comes, that very day
I know you and Gram will show me the way.

Happy Birthday, Rose
With Love from Mom and Saki

Rose Hometchko

3/26/71 - 6/17/09
HAPPY BIRTHDAY

I can never feel alone or separated from you, especially on your birthday. The private moments are the times I am reminded we are never apart because your spirit will live deep within my heart. Saki remembers most of the lessons you taught him. He is now a part of both of us. He is a connection of the tender care of your love for birds. My yesterdays make my tomorrows easier since your spirit lives deep within me. My life is more purposeful and rich in so many ways because of you. You taught me so much about the world that I didn't even think to explore and we did it together. Some people think I am wrong to call your name and speak as though are present, but why, because you are not visible should I dismiss the existence of the time you shared with me here while you were visible? Families are forever and will remain together through eternity. Gram, You and Me will be together once again.

Forever, Rose's Mom

Happy Birthday, Rose

Four years ago we celebrated your birthday at Theo's Metro.
You had a smile and wonderful news to tell me.
A few days ago you were given the second report – "Remission."
You just needed to build your strength.
Happiness dissipated less than a week later.
Hospital admission to Jefferson forced your disbelief.

When you asked to go to Jefferson I was relieved.
You squeezed my hand when you got there.
Somehow you thought I exaggerated my experiences there.
But you realized in a short time the wonderful care they gave,
Especially when doctors called you at the Bed and Breakfast.
I was told, but not you, that you were not in remission.

I miss not being able to hug and kiss you.
Just to hear your voice would give me such joy.
So now I have a multitude of memories to keep me company.
And then there is Saki! Yes, just like Scooter, he is spoiled.
Your spirit or energy lives on in us, in the universe.

You gave so much to others, I am sure changed them.
So, yes, you will always be remembered.
I feel your presence around me every day.
So many memories of places we went and things we did together.
Part of me is with you; part of you is with me.

Forever Entwined.
Love, Mom and Saki